EULOGY WORKBOOK

A STEP-BY-STEP GUIDE TO HELP YOU

WRITE AN UNFORGETTABLE EULOGY

A.V. O'CONNELL

Copyright © 2021 by [AV O'Connell]

All Rights Reserved.

No part of this workbook may be used or reproduced by any means, graphic, electronic, or mechanical, including photocopying, recording, taping, or by any information storage retrieval system without the written permission of the publisher except in the case of brief quotations embodied in critical articles and reviews.

ISBN 978-0-578-94878-2

[Publisher Website (https://eulogyworkbook.com)]

This workbook was birthed from the eulogy of my beloved Auntie and is dedicated to her memory, a kind, humble and generous woman.

Auntie 1950-2021

Celebrating

The Life & Legacy

of

_____

Born On

_____

Departed On

_____

Contents

Foreword

TELL THEIR STORY 1

EIGHT PILLARS TO A STELLAR EULOGY 3

PILLAR ONE EULOGY INTRODUCTION 4

WHAT YOU WILL NEED 7

PILLAR TWO BIRTH, FAMILY & CHILDHOOD 12

PILLAR THREE MILESTONES & ACCOMPLISHMENTS 18

PILLAR FOUR REVELATION - MYSTERY UNVEILED 25

PILLAR FIVE AMPLIFY SALIENT QUALITIES 31

PILLAR SIX UNEXPECTED TURN OF EVENTS 39

PILLAR SEVEN THE GOLDEN YEARS 45

PILLAR EIGHT DECLINING YEARS & SUNSET 51

CONGRATULATIONS! 58

FULL EULOGY EXAMPLE & COMPLETION 59

YOU DID A SPECTACULAR JOB! 88

Foreword

On June 26th, 1969, a step for man and a giant leap for mankind's famous quote, was heralded to the world. But just 21 years later an even bigger step for mankind was taken. It would take over 1000 scientists, from six nations and $3 billion for this monumental and historical project.

The U.S population at the time, had climbed to just over 282 million and the world population was just over 6 billion. Bill Clinton was President. Mad Cow disease was on a rampage across Europe and Y2K retreated into oblivion. The year 2000 was the beginning of the new millennium, the dawn of a new era. An international team of researchers was charting a new voyage of discovery. But this would not be to the cosmos or space exploration, they were going to do something far more remarkable, something unthinkable, something unimaginable – they were going to attempt to sequence or map out the entire human genome!

From the East Room of the White House on 26th, June 2000, President Bill Clinton would announce to the world these famous words, "Today, we are learning the language in which God created life."

In his speech, he said, "We have pooled the combined wisdom of biology, chemistry, physics, engineering, mathematics, and computer science; tapped the great strengths and insights of the public and private sectors. More than 1,000 researchers across six nations have revealed nearly all 3 billion letters of our miraculous genetic code. I congratulate all of you on this stunning and humbling achievement." - President Bill Clinton

So, what exactly did the Human Genome Project discover? It is mind-boggling, so hold on! Wrapped up like a ball of yarn, in the infinitesimally microscopic, tiny nucleus of each cell within our body, they found the actual blueprint of human life!

Three (3.2) billion letters long, it took 13 years to unravel and map out the code that created you and me. The DNA information in just one cell in our body, when stretched out would be 6 ft long. Unravel the DNA in all the cells of one person, it would stretch 10 billion miles, from here to the Sun and back 600 times! Think about that for a moment. Sounds inconceivable, doesn't it?

Even now, scientists continue to learn and unravel new information. The four-letter biological code (A, C, T, and G) of our genome is structured in billions of arrangements, and researchers have yet to understand the meaning or specific instruction of each arrangement. So where did this language come from that is housed in the nucleus of our cells? This blueprint built our bodies cell by cell in the womb, runs every biological process, and keeps us alive. Its complexity is breathless! The information it contains is inexhaustible.

So how should we interpret this finding?

Simply this. Information in whatever form we find it always comes from an intelligent source. Whether it is a headline in a newspaper, a paragraph in a book, a hieroglyphic inscription, an app, a website, or the cryptic codes of World War II – Wherever we find information, we can trace it back to its original source. At the place of its origin, we will **_always_** find "the mind or the intelligence" who created it.

So where did this amazing, infinite information, in our cells come from? Would it be fair to say the "Creator" of life?

I would like to introduce you to God Almighty the Creator of the Universe, the Creator of life, the Creator of you and me. Like parents who are inextricably tied to their biological children, so too, in the same way, God is tied to us, his creation. He loves us more than we can imagine. The question now should be, if God loves us so much, why does he allow us to grow old and die?

That is a good question, and it deserves not just a good answer, but God's answer!

What if, here on Earth, everyone loved each other? No stealing, no lying, no murder, no adultery, no cheating, no death. What if all neighborhoods were safe and peaceful? The flowers brilliant in color, the vegetation lush and abundant. No pollution, no weapons of mass destruction, and the nation's leaders were real friends. Is it Utopia? No, it is the Kingdom of Heaven on Earth. In the oldest manuscript found in the dead sea scrolls, written by the prophet Isaiah, he foretells about such a time in earth's future, when no one will bring harm in all the world!

"Nothing will hurt or destroy in all my holy mountain," God says, "For as the waters fill the sea, so shall the earth be full of the knowledge of the Lord." Isaiah 11:9. So when is this time coming? When Jesus returns! Jesus Christ asks us to pray for it. "Thy Kingdom come on Earth as it is in Heaven!" Matthew 9:6,10.

We are still in the age of the original sin from Genesis, that resulted in the gradual death and decay of our world including the human body. But in the future millions of people will be raised from the dead and will live in the coming Kingdom under the rulership of the King of all kings, Jesus Christ!

When Jesus, Son of God, was faced with the death of a close friend. He wept. Why did He weep? Because death was never His Father's will for humanity. Jesus himself is the rescue plan God initiated to reinstate eternal life to humanity. The famous Bible verse John 3:16 reminds us of this; For God so loved the world he gave his only begotten son, that whoever believes in him (Jesus Christ) should not perish but have eternal life.

Jesus in the presence of a grieving sister who had lost her brother, said to her, "I am the resurrection and life. Those who believe in me even if they die, will never perish but have eternal life." After comforting her with these words, he did the unexpected. Jesus called Lazarus from the grave and brought him back to life! He promises to do it for millions in the future.

Today there are more nuclear weapons to destroy the world many times over. There is much poverty, sickness, death, unscrupulous leaders, corrupt governments in every place. We can all agree, the nations' leaders have not done a good job of creating a righteous, peaceful, and prosperous government for all the citizens of earth. Even now, the drumbeat of World War III echoes in the backdrop of our daily lives. The good news is this, citizenship into the coming Kingdom of Heaven is open to all people from every nation on earth!

As people from all over the world accept Jesus' atonement for their sins, repent from ungodly deeds, and turn to God, their names are being recorded in heaven as citizens of God's coming government. Jesus Christ paid the price for your citizenship into his righteous and peaceful Kingdom that is coming soon. You simply need to believe Jesus and accept His offer of eternal life!

And this my friend, is good news!

God has indeed taken care of the "death" issue and given us the promise of eternal life through his Son Jesus Christ. God is giving us the opportunity to experience living on earth, in a perfect, righteous government in the Kingdom of Heaven. This is God's answer for everyone in the world today, including you and me.

Compassionately Yours,
A. V. O'Connell

Tell Their Story

We prayed fervently with the greatest expectation she would survive. She lasted 33 days in the hospital and then… she was gone! I could still hear her voice and see her smile. The memories came crashing like waves on the shores of my mind. Like a rollercoaster ride, one minute I was smiling, thinking of her, another, I was hurled into a place of despair as the reality of her death plunged me into tears. I would not see her again, at least not on this side of life. I was grieving, and so was everyone else in our family.

No one was prepared to write her eulogy. Her granddaughter said she would, and then she could not. Then they asked me. First, I was shocked. Then I felt so blessed to be given the opportunity to honor my beloved aunt in her passing. I had never written a eulogy before, so the task was nerve-wracking. What would I say? How can I comfort her children, her siblings, and her friends? Then, inspiration came. Just tell her story, like a mini-biography. "Hmm… I could do that," I thought. And that is exactly what I did.

What I discovered in the process, a life story is simply the most powerful, and fitting way we can honor our loved ones in death. Everyone's story is worth telling with all the twists and turns, the mountains, valleys, the challenges, the victories, the good times, and the bad, encapsulated in a poignant short biography, will undoubtedly bring tears, joy, smiles, and even laughter.

Everyone's life has impacted many. Parents, spouses, children, relatives, in-laws, colleagues, neighbors, and friends can speak about the impact just this one person, has had on their lives.

So how exactly can you pull off a memorable and emotionally impactful eulogy flawlessly? If you are thinking you might not be able to accomplish this. Do not worry, we will do it together!

Eight Pillars

to a Stellar Eulogy

You will need eight pillars to create an honorable and most excellent tribute. In this workbook, we will go over each pillar and the components you will use to create a dynamic, and unforgettable eulogy. We will also look at my aunt's eulogy so you can have a guidepost to follow. This workbook will take you step-by-step to help you deliver a memorable eulogy that will be remembered and cherished for years.

So how did my aunt's eulogy turn out? After reading it, the Funeral Director penned these words, *"Your Eulogy was simply beautiful and outstanding and I'm sure that your family will be more than happy, they would feel incredibly proud and honored that you gave a fitting tribute to an outstanding lady who meant everything to so many people. You are all indeed very blessed to have known her."*

There is no doubt in my mind, you too will do an incredible job in creating a stellar and unforgettable eulogy for your loved one! Without further delay let us get started.

To begin we will start with the Introduction.

Pillar One

Eulogy Introduction

Firstly, it should not be boring! It is important to jolt your audience out of their grief and bring them into a happier time. Grab their attention! Make their minds come alive with an emotionally charged introduction that will make them want to listen intently and forget their sadness, for the moment.

Travel back in time into your loved one's past. Find something remarkable, something funny, something memorable, or a challenge they overcame.

If you do not have enough material to work with, that is okay. Simply ask family members, what was most meaningful to them about your now deceased family member. They will have lots of moments to share with you! Make sure you have your phone handy to record everything they say. Why is this so important? You will pick up the inflection in their voices, the tone, and the accompanying emotions tied to the event. This will be invaluable as you paint with your brush stroke every nuance pertinent to their story, the beauty of the life they lived, and their legacy.

Eulogy Introduction

Example #1

There she stood, with a fashionable flair and a small black handbag on her left arm as she posed with the most joyous smile. Strong and proud at her sister's wedding, a symbol of youthful vibrancy in the years gone by. Her sister Jen was 23 and Samantha was just 21. That happy occasion shared with close family and friends was captured and frozen in time. You can still find that portrait, prominently displayed on her oldest sister's living room wall today. A beauty queen in her own right with the infamous updo of the 70's she wore so well. But that was 49 years ago. Samantha, Diana Brachman, adoringly, known by all as "Auntie" became a formidable force and a tower of strength to her children and grandchildren throughout the years.

This is Samantha's story, and her family would like to say thanks so much for joining us in this time of bereavement, as we remember our beloved Auntie, a mother, a daughter, grandmother, sister, aunt, cousin, niece, and friend, but most importantly, a child of our Heavenly Father.

Eulogy Introduction

Example #2

As we made the mile and a half journey on our walk home from school, pools of water were everywhere. A torrential downpour had brought a flash flood at the end of the school day. All of us kids watched with excitement mixed with heart-pounding fear, as tree branches, bottles, and debris were carried with ferocious velocity down the winding trench at the side of the road.

Then suddenly without warning, we were shocked by the most horrific scream! One of the children fell in! The fast-moving water had encased her, taking her to a watery grave. Then my cousin Mike, like Superman leaped in the savage and untamed water and without fear for his safety, saved her! His heroism that day landed him in the local newspapers. He was only ten, but his bravery would be forever remembered by the family whose little girl he saved and the entire community. That was 55 years ago. That first act of heroism propelled Mike into a life journey of saving others. As a world-war II veteran, he again risked his own life to fight for the freedoms we enjoy today. As a firefighter, he battled many fires saving lives again and again.

This is Michael John O'Leary's story. In our time of bereavement, we would like to thank everyone for joining us to celebrate his life and his legacy.

What You Will Need

First, collect the information. You can use material from your memory, or ask family members, co-workers, and friends for their memories. Remember to record on your phone, what they tell you. Once you have compiled recordings, select the one you will use for the introduction. Then use the workbook to jot down the details of the account you would like to use. All the recordings you have compiled will be important to bring their story together. You will need most, if not all of them later as you move through the next seven pillars.

Write Your Pillar One Here

Eulogy Introduction

Eulogy Introduction

Eulogy Introduction

Pillar Two

Birth, Family & Childhood

As the wings slowly break free from the wall of its silky encasement, a butterfly, once a humble caterpillar, is lifted to a new dimension, emerges in a beautiful array of colors to add its beauty and wonder to our world. And so too is the arrival of a newborn child! Every story begins with birth. Events surrounding birth, parents, and family are what make everyone's story ever so interesting. Often, the people we become were in direct correlation to the children we were, and the events that helped shape and determined our lives. Was there any childhood sickness? How did she/he interact with siblings? Was your loved one shy, outgoing, quiet, or a loudmouth? As your family meets to celebrate their life, these events, and the people that helped made them possible, people who will be sitting in the audience will be greatly blessed to relive some of these memories they shared with the deceased. Find family members like parents and siblings that can speak on a personal level about your loved one's childhood. This will provide a good first-hand experience for you to chronicle the beginning of their life's journey.

Birth, Family & Childhood

Example

Born on September 26th, 1950, to John and Ruth Fenton, (known as Grandpa Jay and Nina) Samantha, Diana Brachman was the 9th of ten children. She was an adorable plump and happy child. Her mom Nina would recall how people were always drawn towards her beautiful little girl. Her infectious smile and sweet spirit were appealing to everyone. Nina said, "It all changed with the Polio vaccine." No disease frightened parents like polio did. The vaccine brought hope. But for Samantha, the vaccine was tragic - it impacted her rather badly and caused cognitive delays that impaired her in so many ways. The vaccine damage would forever change her life and close doors of opportunity, most take for granted. But Samantha was a fighter, and not a victim to anything, or anyone. She strived with a can-do attitude and a vivacious tenacity that would make her into the woman we have all come to know and love.

Write Your Pillar Two Here

Birth, Family & Childhood

Birth, Family & Childhood

Birth, Family & Childhood

Pillar Three

Milestones & Accomplishments

Milestones and accomplishments, from birth to death, are sprinkled throughout our lives. They create a beautiful tapestry interwoven with peaks, valleys, and shades of colors depicting life's ups and downs. They are our mountain top and valley experiences and are inextricably tied to challenges and victories. Battles fought and won through blood, sweat, tears, joy, and lots of laughter. They are what makes life truly profound and create dynamic legacies. Our first love, graduating from college, leaving home, the first job, the first car, getting married, overcoming tragedy, starting a business, and so much more. As children, our parents cataloged our milestones, but as adults, we tend not to. However, milestones and accomplishments are pivotal in your loved one's story and will become a part of their legacy. Talk with others to discover major milestones and accomplishments as you build out their eulogy.

Milestones & Accomplishments

Example #1

She was a vibrant and carefree young woman at 21. She had just moved away from home when she met the love of her life. After a long and challenging courtship, in 1983, at 33 years of age, Samantha, Diana Fenton, was joined in holy matrimony to Jacob, Joseph Brachman (better known as Joe). Their family was blessed with 4 boys, Mark, (known as Lil Joe), Anthony, Charles, and Bobby. And one little princess, Julia.

Author's note: My aunt was a career mom and grandmother. The role she played in her family was her greatest and most cherished accomplishment. This is what made her so loved by all.

Milestones & Accomplishments

Example #2

Mike was not an academic genius, but he was obsessed with repairing cars. He could diagnose your car problem by just listening to the engine. In 1941, after failing most of his finals, Mike, would not consider repeating the 12th grade, so he enlisted into the U.S Army. Just a few months later, Japan bombed Pearl Harbor and dragged the U.S into World War II. After basic training, Mike became a pilot of a B-24 bomber and was stationed in Old Buckenham, England where he ran bombing missions over Nazi-occupied Europe. He piloted 35 missions with a near miss of being shot down on his last one over Salzburg, Austria, as they prepared the city for U.S troops to enter on May 5th, 1945. After being discharged in 1945, Mike worked as a firefighter and subsequently was promoted to fire chief. Two years later June 25th, 1947, Mike was honored by President Harry S. Truman with the purple heart medal for saving his platoon from enemy fire during his last mission. Mike married Elizabeth Mc Govern his high school sweetheart in 1949. They were blessed with two daughters, Janice, and Patricia.

Write Your Pillar Three Here

Milestones & Accomplishments

Milestones & Accomplishments

Milestones & Accomplishments

Pillar Four

Revelation - Mystery Unveiled

Have you ever wondered how someone came to be known by their nickname? I can guarantee there is a pretty darn interesting story behind it, and it is worth telling. Pillar Four can be composed of anything most family and friends never knew about your loved one. Maybe it is the time they backpacked across Europe with no money. It could be their altruism, and how they quietly supported orphans in China.

Maybe they wrote and published a few novels that never really took off, so they never mentioned it. Whatever the mystery is, make sure it will amplify the story you are telling about your loved one. It should be a compliment and a pleasant surprise! It should make everyone smile or bring comfort and happy feelings to those listening. Keep in mind, their eulogy will also be chronicled as a part of the "order of service" booklet. This will be a part of their legacy and become a keepsake for all in attendance. Happy discovery as you uncover something remarkable and that pleasant surprise!

Revelation - Mystery Unveiled

Example

So, the Big Question? How did Samantha become Auntie? The secret is with Lil Joe her firstborn, who, as a little tot decided he would copy his cousin, Jacklyn who was 3 years older and called his mom, Auntie like she did! He followed her further by calling his Aunt Jen, Mommy. Twisted, isn't it? Blame it all on Lil Joe, because when his siblings came along, they followed their older brother, and they too called their mom, Auntie. What is more hilarious, they all called their Aunt Jen Mommy! Not only did Samantha's children called their mom Auntie, so did everyone else. So, from the Montiga to England, America, and beyond, Samantha, Diana Brachman was now famously known as Auntie!

Write Your Pillar Four Here

Revelation – Mystery Unveiled

Revelation – Mystery Unveiled

Revelation – Mystery Unveiled

Pillar Five

Amplify Salient Qualities

What made your loved ones who they were? What notable character traits best defined them? How would most remember them? Were they selfless in giving? Were they a go-getter with defiance against obstacles? Were they resolved and composed with great thinking ability? Whatever their notable traits were, you want to amplify them in Pillar Five with a couple of stories or examples. What you will find as you complete Pillar Five, you will have to talk about persons and/or family members who were directly involved in your loved one's story. Chances are these persons or family members will be in the audience as the eulogy is being read. You cannot imagine the emotional driver this is! The honorable mention of their names in your loved one's memoir will cause them to laugh, some will cry, but it will be a feeling of solace and comfort. It will be such an honor for them to be a part of the celebration of their deceased loved one's life!

Pillar Five Example

Amplify Salient Qualities

Auntie was a stern, no-nonsense kind of parent. Discipline was prompt and sometimes intense. Bad behavior was never tolerated. Yet her love for her children was unquestionable. She worked tirelessly to provide for their needs and was an anchor for her family. Travel with me back in time for a moment and you will see what I mean.

It was a typical hot Saturday afternoon. It was the family's baking day, and the smell of Auntie's bread filled the yard. Everyone was at Grandma Nina's to share in this weekly family tradition. As the adults baked, chatted, and laughed in the background, we kids were watching Anthony, the master coconut slayer, rip a coconut to shreds with a machete. He could not be more than eight years old. But he was certain he could get the job done. We believed him! Every chop was getting him closer to the nut… And then…. the unthinkable, the scream! "O Ga! Oh Ga! Oh Ga! Oh Ga!" was all I heard and watched Anthony leaping, with blood spouting through the air! His Thumb was gone! Auntie hearing her son hollering, made a mad dash to his rescue! She found Anthony's thumb on the ground! She wrapped his hand in a towel, and in a flash was at St. Mary's Hospital to save her son! How she got from the country to the city so fast is still a mystery to me! She was like Super Mom on steroids! Just ask Anthony, He will tell you, "My mother, she will always be my hero. "

Author's note: Her son was in the audience as well as other family members who were there during this traumatic event. As they relived the moment, this recollection brought much laughter and smiles. Here is another event, that amplifies my aunt's parenting style.

Mark known as Lil Joe, her firstborn would say, "Auntie, my mom amazes me and she did not play." He tells about the time he got his first job as a young lad. Payday came. everyone got a check, but Lil Joe got nothing! Lil Joe was too nervous to ask the boss man for his money! So, home he went to Auntie with his head hung low. Auntie expected Lil Joe to have his paycheck! When Auntie **found out that the boss man did not pay** Lil Joe, **Auntie could not believe her ears! She immediately took** Lil Joe back to the worksite to find the boss man. She confronted him about her son's pay. The lying crook, said, "I paid him his money." But Lil Joe said, "Auntie he didn't pay me. He paid everyone else." About the same time, Auntie's eyes landed on a stack of white envelopes in the boss man's shirt pocket. She dragged them out of his pocket and spread them out in front of him and behold there was Lil Joe's envelope with his name on It! She took Lil Joe's envelope out of the stack and back slapped the boss man in his chest! She sternly said to the boss man, "When my son works for you, you pay him his money!" And home Auntie and Lil Joe went with his check! Lil Joe left with his mom that day thinking, "My Mom is the "REAL" boss!" Lil Joe too would tell you, "My Mom, Auntie, for certain will always be my hero!"

Write Your Pillar Five Here

Amplify Salient Qualities

Amplify Salient Qualities

Amplify Salient Qualities

Pillar Six

Unexpected Turn of Events

Every life, every person has had or will have them at some point throughout their life. The unexpected turn of events that changes everything! Remember Hurricane Katrina the category five storm in 2005 that caused 1,800 deaths, $125 billion in damages? It wreaked havoc across the city of New Orleans and brought devastation of historic proportions.

Many lives were suddenly uprooted as homes were lost to flooding and category five winds. So many became displaced and had to move to other states. They were forced to start all over again. Whether it is a natural disaster, a financial loss, a failed marriage, an untimely death of a loved one, or sickness, the unexpected, can dramatically alter destinies and change the course of one's life. But it is not what life throws at us that makes stories memorable and impactful, rather is how we respond and overcome the unexpected. Your loved one had their own unexpected events they overcame. How they overcame the setback is a story worth telling. Many will be touched by it!

Unexpected Turn of Events

Example

In July 1995, La Montiga Hills volcano, dormant for centuries, erupted and buried the island's capital. Two years later, on October 22nd, 1997, due to eruption Auntie along with her family and her ailing mother (diagnosed with terminal cancer) migrated to the United Kingdom. Almost immediately she found another Methodist Church and became an integral part of the women's fellowship. Kingsley Methodist Church was a bedrock for the family in a new and strange land. As grandchildren were born, Auntie made sure they too would join and the rest of the family in regular fellowship at Kinsley.

Then, sadly Nina her beloved mother's health failed. Doctors could do no more, and an option was given to place her mom in a care home. Auntie defiantly objected. Along with Joe and the rest of the family, Auntie faithfully took care of her mother until Jan 20th, 2001, when her beloved mother Ruth Nina Fenton took her last breath and went to be with Lord.

Write Your Pillar Six Here

Unexpected Turn of Events

Unexpected Turn of Events

Unexpected Turn of Events

Pillar Seven

The Golden Years

Sometimes they are referred to as "empty nesters", seniors, retirees, or elderly, but to their grandchildren, they are grandpa and grandma or "granny" if you are British. If your loved one is over the age of 65, you would want to include 'The Golden Years'. Most likely your loved one has raised children, attended graduations and weddings, traveled, plant gardens, and taken up hobbies to keep busy as life started winding down.

How can you bring their golden years to life with meaning and warmth? Were they active? Did they volunteer in the community? On a more somber note, these years may include sickness and hospitalization. How did they overcome the illness? How about their advice and the role they played in imparting wisdom to others in their family? Think about how meaningful these years were to those whom they impacted during their golden years. The richness and beauty of these years should be celebrated – Assuredly, family members will be touched.

The Golden Years

Example

Over the years as Auntie grew older her relationship with God deepened and the once rough edges of her personality softened into a meek and gentle spirit. Prayer became a powerful part of her daily life. When I called Auntie to check-in to see how she was doing, she would always say, "I prayed for all of you, I called everyone by name this morning." Auntie would spend the time to cover every family member and their household, praying for God's mercy and blessing on their lives. She would even pray for the airplanes passing overhead. She would say, "Lord take them safely to their destination." In 2017 when she collapsed and was rushed to the hospital, Auntie was in critical condition. Her heart stopped for 17 minutes. Family poured into the hospital from across London; The prayers were non-stop in America, and the Montiga pleading with God for recovery and God heard and answered. Her commitment to praying for us was returned to her as copious showers of blessing in God's merciful extension of her life.

Write Your Pillar Seven Here

The Golden Years

The Golden Years

The Golden Years

Pillar Eight

Declining Years & Sunset

Across the western sky, just above the horizon, breathtaking hues of reds, pink, and orange waltz gracefully on stage as they appear for a curtain call. It is the end of the day and like the sands of an hourglass, sunsets represent Pillar Eight, the closing chapter of their story. Savor and capture the moment of picturesque beauty, for sunsets are captivating but soon disappear behind the horizon, eclipsed, and engulfed by nightfall. Similarly, our lives mirror the fleeting hours of sunset as we move closer towards the final days of our lives.

Because this part of the eulogy will remind your audience, of the reason they have gathered, and the passing of their loved one, take the time to carefully bring beauty, and grace to this part of the eulogy. A sense of peace and closure should wash over them as they listen to the end of the eulogy. The life lived is gone, but their memory and their legacy will last forever in the minds and hearts of their loved ones left behind.

Declining Years & Sunset

Example

God gave us three more precious years with Auntie. She recovered, but never returned to her former self. As her health continued to decline, her son Bobby became her support. And even with all her health issues, Auntie by God's grace beat Covid-19 and cheated death again! However, on April 07th, 2021, she collapsed at home and was hospitalized for a little over a month. Again, the prayers and pleading for her life were lifted to heaven to save her once more, but this time, she would not return to us. Auntie quietly departed this life at 9:30 pm on Sunday, May 9th, 2021, at Hamilton University Hospital and peacefully joined her sister Margaret (Pinky) Fenton, and her parents.

Her 70 years in Montiga and the U.K, although challenging at times are filled with a rich tapestry of precious memories of Samantha Diana Fenton-Bachman, "Our Beloved Auntie" that can never be forgotten.

Auntie's beautiful life will forever be cherished in the lives of her children Mark, Anthony, Charles, Julia, and Bobby; Three brothers; Luke, William, and Jonathan; Two sisters LouAnne and

Jen, thirteen grandchildren; ten great-grandchildren, and a host of nieces, nephews, cousins, loved ones, and friends.

Rest in the arms of Jesus our beloved Auntie! We love you... until we meet again.

Your family will forever feel your presence in our hearts!

Write Your Pillar Eight Here

Declining Years & Sunset

Declining Years & Sunset

Declining Years & Sunset

Congratulations!

You have stuck it out and have completed all eight pillars! Now it is time to bring it together for a memorable and beautiful eulogy for your loved one. On the next page, you will find a copy of my aunt's full eulogy. Hopefully, you will find it helpful.

Author's note: All names and places in my aunt's eulogy have been changed for the privacy and respect of my beloved aunt and our family.

Full Eulogy

Example

There she stood, with a fashionable flair and a small black handbag on her left arm as she posed with the most joyous smile. Strong and proud at her sister's wedding, a symbol of youthful vibrancy in the years gone by. Her sister Jen was 23 and Samantha was just 21. That happy occasion shared with close family and friends was captured and frozen in time. You can still find that portrait, prominently displayed on her oldest sister's living room wall today. A beauty queen in her own right with the infamous updo of the 70's she wore so well. But that was 49 years ago. Samantha, Diana Brachman, adoringly, known by all as "Auntie" became a formidable force and a tower of strength to her children and grandchildren throughout the years.

This is Samantha Bachman's story, and her family would like to say thanks for joining us in this time of bereavement, as we remember our beloved Auntie, a mother, a daughter, grandmother, sister, aunt, cousin, niece, and friend, but most importantly, a child of our Heavenly Father.

Born on September 26th, 1950, to John and Ruth Fenton, (known as Grandpa Jay and Nina) Samantha, Diana Brachman was the 9th of ten children. She was an adorable plump and happy child. Her mom Nina would recall how people were always drawn towards her beautiful little girl. Her infectious smile and sweet spirit were appealing to everyone. Nina said, "It all changed with the Polio vaccine." No disease frightened parents like polio did. The vaccine brought hope. But for Samantha, the vaccine was tragic. It impacted her rather badly and caused cognitive delays that impaired her in so many ways. The vaccine damage would forever change her life and close doors of opportunity, most take for granted. But Samantha was a fighter, and not a victim to anything, or anyone. She strived with a can-do attitude and a vivacious tenacity that would make her into the woman we have all come to know and love.

Samantha was a vibrant and carefree young woman in her late twenties when she moved away from home. She finally met the love of her life at thirty. After a rocky courtship, in 1983, at 33 years of age, Samantha, Diana Fenton, was joined in holy matrimony to Jacob, Joseph Brachman (better known as Joe).

Their family was blessed with four boys, Mark, (known as Lil Joe), Anthony, Charles, and Bobby. And one little princess, Julia.

So, the Big Question? How did Samantha become Auntie? The secret is with Lil Joe her firstborn, who, as a little tot decided he would copy his cousin, Jacklyn who was 3 years older and called his mom, Auntie like she did. He followed her further by calling his Aunt Jen, Mommy. Twisted, isn't it? Blame it all on Lil Joe, because when his siblings came along, they followed their older brother, and they too called their mom, Auntie. What is more hilarious, they all called their Aunt Jen Mommy! Not only did Samantha's children called her Auntie, everyone else did also.

So, from Montiga Island to England, America, and beyond, Samantha, Diana Brachman was now famously known as Auntie.

Auntie was a stern, no-nonsense kind of parent. Discipline was prompt and sometimes intense. Bad behavior was never tolerated. Yet her love for her children was unquestionable. She worked tirelessly to provide for their needs and was an anchor for her family. Travel with me back in time for a moment and you will see what I mean.

It was a typical hot Saturday afternoon. It was the family's baking day, and the smell of Auntie's bread filled the yard. Everyone was at Grandma Nina's to share in this weekly family tradition. As the adults baked, chatted, and laughed in the background, we kids were watching Anthony, the master coconut slayer, rip a coconut to shreds with a machete. He could not be more than eight years old. But he was certain he could get the job done. We believed him! Every chop was getting him closer to the nut… And then…. the unthinkable, the scream! "O Ga! Oh Ga! Oh Ga! Oh Ga!" **was all I heard and watched Anthony leaping, with blood spouting through the air. His thumb was gone! Auntie hearing her** son hollering, made a mad dash to his rescue! She found Anthony's thumb on the ground! She wrapped his hand in a towel, and in a flash was at St. Mary's Hospital to save her son! How she got from the country to the city so fast is still a mystery to me! She was like Super Mom on steroids! Just ask Anthony what he thinks about his mom. He will tell you, "My mother, she will always be my hero!"

Mark known as Lil Joe, her firstborn would say, "Auntie, my mom amazes me, and she did not play!" He tells about the time he got his first job as a young lad. Payday came. Everyone got a check, but Lil Joe got nothing! Lil Joe was too nervous to ask the boss man for his money! So, home he went to Auntie with his head hung low. Auntie expected Lil Joe to have his paycheck! When Auntie found out that the boss man did not pay Lil Joe, Auntie could not believe her ears! She immediately took Lil Joe back to the worksite to find the boss man. She confronted him about her son's pay. The lying crook, said, "I paid him his money." But Lil Joe said, "Auntie he didn't pay me. He paid everyone else." About the same time, Auntie's eyes landed on a stack of white envelopes in the boss man's shirt pocket.

She dragged them out of his pocket and spread them out in front of him and behold there was Lil Joe's envelope with his name on It! She took Lil Joe's envelope out of the stack and back slapped the boss man in his chest! She sternly said to the boss man, "When my son works for you, you pay him his money!" And home Auntie and Lil Joe went with his check! Lil Joe left with his mom that day thinking, "My Mom is the "REAL" boss!" Lil Joe too would tell you, "My Mom, Auntie, for certain will always be my hero!"

Auntie's upbringing and her mother's example provided the foundation for her faith in God. Attending weekly church services with her family at Hill Rock Methodist Church was pivotal in raising her children to fear God and live right. As an active member of the church, she contributed significantly through her love of baking and took much pride in presenting her best gift on behalf of her family at harvest time.

In July 1990, La Montiga Hills volcano, dormant for centuries, erupted and buried the island's capital. Two years later, on October 22nd, 1992, due to the eruption, Auntie along with her family and her ailing mother (diagnosed with terminal cancer) migrated to the United Kingdom. Almost immediately she found another Methodist Church and became an integral part of the women's fellowship. Kingsley Methodist Church was a bedrock for the family in a new and strange land. As grandchildren were born, Auntie made sure they too would join and the rest of the family in regular fellowship at Kinsley.

Then, sadly Nina, her beloved mother's health failed. Doctors could do no more, and an option was given to place her mom in a care home. Auntie defiantly objected. Along with Joe and the rest of the family, Auntie faithfully took care of her mother until

Jan 20th, 2001, when her beloved mother, Ruth Nina Fenton took her last breath and went to be with Lord.

With Nina gone, Auntie turned her heart of gold to her eldest sister LouAnne who was getting along in years and living alone. She would take four buses and almost two hours to get to her sister each week. Auntie brought her cooked meals, cleaned, and spend time reminiscing about the good ole days in Montiga. Her sister LouAnne looked forward to seeing Auntie and the warmth her visits brought to her heart.

Auntie was much loved by all her grandchildren, and she loved them even more! We implored her to stay in America with us during her 2014 visit, but she missed hearing the word "Granny" and the little voice of Matthew on a phone call, saying "Granny I miss you, I miss your porridge" melted her heart. As an endearing gesture of her fondness and love, she would add "Oh" to their names. "Matt-Ohhh and Lini-Ohhh" she would say. Today, this sweet memory of their grandmother is forever etched in their hearts and her beautiful voice will always remain a part of them.

Among their most cherished memories was their grandmother's house filled with her entire family on Sundays. Auntie, they recalled, would cook up a feast fit for a king. She would then get

all the children ready and take them with her to church. They laughed as they remember how Granny as soon as she got to the door would always forget something and had to go back in the house for her keys or bus pass.

Over the years as Auntie grew older her relationship with God deepened and the once rough edges of her personality softened into a meek and gentle spirit. Prayer became a powerful part of her daily life. When I called Auntie to check-in to see how she was doing, she would always say, "I prayed for all of you, I called everyone by name this morning." Auntie would spend the time to cover every family member and their household, praying for God's mercy and blessing on their lives.

She would even pray for the airplanes passing overhead. She would say, "Lord take them safely to their destination". In 2015 when she collapsed and rushed to the hospital, Auntie was in critical condition. Her heart stopped for 17 minutes. Family poured into the hospital from across London; The prayers were non-stop in America, and Montiga, pleading with God for recovery and God heard and answered. Her commitment to praying for us was returned to her as copious showers of blessing in God's merciful extension of her life.

God gave us three more precious years with Auntie. She recovered, but never returned to her former self. As her health continued to decline, her son Bobby became her support. And even with all her health issues, Auntie by God's grace beat Covid-19 and cheated death again! However, on April 07th, 2021, she collapsed at home and was hospitalized for a little over a month. Again, the prayers and pleading for her life were lifted to heaven to save her once more, but this time, she would not return to us.

Auntie quietly departed this life at 9:30 pm on Sunday, May 9th, 2021, at Jefferson University Hospital and peacefully joined her sister Margaret (Brownie) Fenton, and her parents.

Her 70 years in Montiga Island and the U.K, although challenging at times are filled with a rich tapestry of precious memories of Samantha Diana Fenton-Bachman, our beloved Auntie that can never be forgotten. Auntie's beautiful life will forever be cherished in the lives of her children Mark, Anthony, Charles,

Julia, and Bobby; Three brothers; Luke, William, and Jonathan; Two sisters LouAnne and Jen Elizabeth, thirteen grandchildren, ten great-grandchildren, and a host of nieces, nephews, cousins, loved ones and friends.

Rest in the arms of Jesus our beloved Auntie! We love you! Until we meet again. We will forever feel your presence in our hearts!

End of Eulogy

Author's note: On the next page you will combine all eight pillars to bring your loved one's life story together. Thank you for allowing me into your family's time of bereavement to assist you with writing your loved one's eulogy.

Begin Your Loved One's Full Eulogy

Full Eulogy Completion

Full Eulogy Completion

Full Eulogy Completion

Full Eulogy Completion

Full Eulogy Completion

Full Eulogy Completion

Full Eulogy Completion

Full Eulogy Completion

Full Eulogy Completion

Full Eulogy Completion

Full Eulogy Completion

Full Eulogy Completion

Full Eulogy Completion

Full Eulogy Completion

Full Eulogy Completion

Full Eulogy Completion

Full Eulogy Completion

You did a spectacular job!

Your family will be both pleased and blessed with such a fitting and full eulogy for your departed loved one. I hope this workbook lived up to your expectations. Read your completed eulogy to three close family members for feedback. They may have a few finishing touches. Always include the eulogy in the "order of service" booklet as it will become a keepsake for most if not all in attendance.

Again, my deepest condolences to you and your loved ones during this time of bereavement. I pray the eulogy you have composed for the funeral services will bring comfort and some peace as you lay your beloved to rest.

Sincerely,

A. V O'Connell

Still Need Help?

With the passing of a loved one, and all the planning a family is faced with, sometimes the task of writing a eulogy can be a tremendous challenge. Many times, families would love to have some help. Should you need someone to help your family write your loved one's eulogy, you may contact help@eulogyworkbook.com

References

(New King James Bible, NKJV,1616/n.d., John 3:16) (Thomas Nelson Inc, 1982, John) (New King James Version, Super Giant Bible New Testament, 2011)

(New King James Bible, NKJV,1616/n.d., Isaiah 11:9) (Thomas Nelson Inc, 1982, Isaiah) (New King James Version, Super Giant Bible Old Testament, 2011)

Heidi Chial, Ph.D. (*Write Science Right*) © 2008 Nature Education.
Citation: Chial, H. (2008) DNA sequencing technologies key to the Human Genome Project. *Nature Education* 1(1):219

Katrin Weigmann The code, the text and the language of God
EMBO Rep. 2004 Feb; 5(2): 116–118. doi: 10.1038/sj.embor.7400069
PMCID: PMC1298980

Nova Online Cracking the Code of life, PBS.
Sources (1-5,7, 15-21) National human Genome
Research Institute Web site; (2) NOVA "Cracking the Code"

A day for the ages, Belief.net; Washington, June 26th, 2000, Archives
https://www.beliefnet.com/news/2000/07/a-day-for-the-ages.aspx

Reading the book of Life, NY, New York Times, June 27th, 2000, text of the White the White House Statements on the Human Genome; Archives,
Https://archive.nytimes.com/www.nytimes.com/library/national/science/062700 sci-genome-text.html

www.ingramcontent.com/pod-product-compliance
Lightning Source LLC
Chambersburg PA
CBHW072015290426
44109CB00018B/2248